Sixty Sexy Sonnets

∞ ∞ ∞

'A Pot of Little Songs'

—From the Quill of—

Jamie Shaw

Paperback: 978-1-964035-04-8
eBook: 978-1-964035-05-5
Library of Congress Control Number: 2024906831

This is a work of nonfiction.

SWEETSPIRE LITERATURE
—— MANAGEMENT ——

*... for Mali, for Ella,
for Eva ...*

'An Ever-Burning Word'

[one]

How am I less unconscionably free
To write of love, if not to write of thee?
I sycophant, I succour, rot, rust, rind,
But scantly merit sampling—at behest!—
A love so exothermic, so inclined
To extricate, in dotage, one from jest...
Pray, take this gift, as rose infecting dew,
As one heart's paltry part to gall preferr'd,
And understand thy song, as sung unto—
A spurning, churning, ever-burning word!
Yet, take me, being pious by design,
And let us be in love, in bed, in thine!

For, lest thou subject be to con or curse,
Thou shalt here resurrection find ... in verse!

'No-Show'

[two]

I pick apart her heart—askew, a loan!—
And, artful grown, nine satin stiches sewn
Pronounce dead at the scene that witch's stone:
My God, why hast thou not forsaken *her*,
And let me take enlightenment to bed?
Pray tell, why must I eat *Bermuda fur*
Mown as a lawn: so coarse, so prickly—dead?
Good Lord, who fishest men, one stitch in time
I'd make to be a Saviour of thine ilk—
Who art so peerless: Consequently I'm
Unfit to spare that holy cow I milk
From sizzling, like a sausage, for her crime!

Disposed am I to call despair my foe,
When dealt a hairless hoax ... no-show below!

'Black Caviar'

[three]

O risen rose, by God so nearly, thou
Art in His peak ubiquity—and how!
His fitful face He'll make to shine upon
Those pit bulls back on Earth (who pine for lawn)—
But *His* love, wholly helpful, dear *Celeste*,
Hath slung thee, safe and sound, to Everest...
Thou art a grain of sand on Heaven's shore
Remotely captivating, all the more
Delightful for its *glitterati* spared—
Concur thou must: a fish He hath ensnared,
Neat angler in the sky, God on a tree,
Whose dying there will be the death—of me!

The last shall be first, to be first put to bed—
Black caviar's better ... but I prefer red!

'Fish Forever'

[four]

I'd follow thee, O zealous, jealous Fish,
To death, should'st thou this of me stern require:
Beelzebub the likes of us would squish
In his rebellion's rude, repugnant mire—
Thy love he shouldn't merit to inspire,
That fell, fallacious, fiendish, foolish liar!
But *thee* to reckon swell, from go to woe,
Who makest bright and beautiful each thing,
Ought cluster clean collusion with the roe
From which thy fill of fishiness did spring—
I shall, *forsooth*, as David, stoop to sling
Encomia to thee, my scaly King!

Thou art supreme, devoid of any fault—
Like pizza with anchovies ... high in salt!

'Motive Cruel, Divine'

[five]

If life its meaning have, divinely view'd,
Doth this effusion, rationally woo'd,
Elude a proposition nude—construed
By scientist, philosopher, or poet—
Lest hours crude be chew'd, on food he brood
In lifetimes lent, t' intuit, guess, or know it...
Whose policy so prim, dear Jim, must swim
T' invent thee, lover leaving on a limb?
Thou doest better asking that of *Him*,
On whose despotic, diabolic whim
Thou be upon this pleasing planet placed—
Antipodes to fathom ... venom laced!

Though thou, on life's concession, be forgot,
To live it wasn't vain, 'tis certain—not!

'Rainbow Lorikeet'

 [six]

Thee, mistress white, might I esteem supreme—
Whose black, aberrant, combinative beam
Hath grey subordination ent'ring seen?
In wisdom's wile, I, caught jester green,
By lilac lust to thee would fain be giv'n,
To fathom, virgin blue, so darkly driv'n,
Those crimson beds, where, clean as kerosene,
I, mean red devil, scant rebounded, burnt,
(So yellow yet of belly, lesson learnt)
Still hope my purple purpose to have earnt!
How now, brown Jersey cow? In courting rhyme,
Do pink carnations toe this lemon's lime?

A rainbow lorikeet's my soul, and yet
The Sun on old Gethsemane hath set!

'Lo, Lamb Lupine, Lost!'

[seven]

To succour sweet treat ardent whim, Fair Rose,
Admitting, in psychotic quarantine,
Its need, this institution of repose
To turn into an orphanage—between
Love's votary, her tender tentacle
Whose *bête* in white so *noire*, she can but squeeze,
To please his canticle: *"Resent a pill*
Not—Diva's keys will prop duopolies!"
'Twere lunacy to tarry, in disgrace
With jolly Jupiter, on hand like grease—
But Saturnine, asleep in outer space,
Is Love for Faith ... impugning lupine fleece!

Angelic voices croon, both in and out
Their blandishment allaying ... through a bout!

'Whole Cream in Vogue'

[eight]

"*Whole cream—is it in Vogue?*" she's posing, sweet,
So pitting souls quiescent (and discrete)
Against their Hippocratic easybeat ...
Whose medicine's for Edison's *élite*!
Conspire just to clean your plastic *rôle*s!
Require lust to glean elastic knolls!
Inspire trust to wean more spastic shoals
Of fire: dust too mean for drastic holes!
Whole cream in Vogue? 'Tis most emphatic end
For milk and sugar to be patted on
A lamington, a trifle, or a scone,
Or else in spurts to meet thee, round the bend—

A caveat however: Do not eat me,
Lest silence come on down ... a clown to beat thee!

'Honey Come Alive'

[nine]

To liberate thy genes, O peach in pink—
To liberate my rod, as sinkers sink
To dread depths dead ... the callous combination!
Thinkers think, philosophizing, rising
Like a baker's bread, like theorizing
Into Heaven's Heights, time stationary...
Very precious, precious, sweet one, peachy
Genes that grope to reach the wrench primeval,
Speaking hues of honey come alive:
Revival's furry fount's her hive, survival's
Knowing vent to *not* come in—her rival's!

Let merit's man inherit fancied flesh,
Dene's dux divining dew on down of dish—
His wanderlust in Lebensraum ... her niche!

'Hopeless Heart'

O Gentle Rose, my friend in direst need,
Whom God from Earthly bondage hath so free'd;
Whom God, in one omnipotent caress,
Did suffer to receive a cranky knife—
Which, sanction'd, in one bloody awful mess,
In squaline feeding frenzy, took thy life:
Thou be not gone, nor vanishèd from here
Can e'er be *rôle* for remnants of thee, Dear—
Thy soul's engraving here on hopeless heart...
For though tactility of being Earth
On whim of dolt (or deity) depart,
A rose, in tender cries, will prize her worth:

In two though chopp'd thy stalk, above a tryst
In lieu co-opt? Why baulk a lover miss'd!

'Artemis'

[eleven]

Thou, Artemis, carriage of casual claim,
So focal and fecund, by artlessness cross'd:
Did ever true cunning make hopefulness lame?
If ever the first of these prosper'd, thou wast
Its owner and advocate—quilling the same
Precursor to palpable Paradise lost,
I rose to thy mettle, my terminal game
To book thy delivery, lovingly toss'd!
Write sonnets, but write them not too many more;
Write twenty, to vary on themes: like the son
Becoming a man to instruct and adore—
To wreck equanimity's longing for one!

In time is no will, save what stirring can wake—
With, in a mound thine, sense unerringly spake!

'Pretty Pennies'

[twelve]

Lock'd in my grain thou shalt forever be,
Ripe Russian vixen, prone to coquetry,
Who, like unto a vision, didst appear
To neither rudely relegate, nor scorn;
Didst seem, indeed, by reasoning unclear,
Unto my poor, prosaic person drawn...
Of thy demeanour vulpine, rich, refined,
Doth recollection harrow to remind—
In that thou, precious angel, slipp'ry asp,
Must so elude predation's dire grasp,
And smile—with a wave from parting tram
To leave the lost still losing ... as I am!

If Fortune's pretty pennies found a purse
In Penury, I'm wond'ring which is worse!

'Like unto a Lemon'

That trek, on this old turning, trembling globe,
Thou should'st like to consider finely mapp'd,
But threadbare, and moth-eaten, is the robe
In which I find thee swaddled—wrapp'd and trapp'd!
If I yet, on this precious, prudent hand,
Construe devotion's notion in a band,
No feud shall, Escapee, get off for free—
Foresight sufficing, Rose, to guarantee
That I am not that doleful deity
Whose cross, crass cant, in cruel propensity,
Is, like unto a lemon, bitter then,
When wars will test salami's salty men

To host a ghost they toast to holy call—
O ye of little faith ... and cannon ball!

'Skin So Even Brown'

[fourteen]

That skin—so even brown, disclosed to all—
My God, I wish it lent not come t' enthral!
Instead, parading naked on her bench,
Secreting not from shame that sticky stench
Of leaking lust, she's taking horns that blow—
To fête *ensemble*'s claim ... to wares on show!
And now torment and torture wrack mine ear,
That she, designing others drawing near,
Denieth not to *honey come alive*
Impartial access to the Queen Bee's hive!
If lust, that bleak imposter, foster truth,
Through *glasnost* must its cost be lost ... in ruth!

For skin, on *femme fatale*, hath booby traps
Her fatally infecting ... just perhaps!

'Toucan'

[fifteen]

Bewitching is birdlife, in absence before,
For now, being lovely here, present the more...
Piranha pernicious, I'm dropping square jaws
At happening hips, willing wily wherefores,
And breasts borne to baffle—as lustre will lurk
In eyes which encase an irreverent smirk,
To climax in cages of cabbage cajoled
By love into being ... too hot to be cold!
Thou, six stirring senses, awakening pleas,
Art heart, here for mentoring, through melodies
Conquistadors conjure, too timorous lest
Their chic Amazonian covet the rest!

Adorning thee, fauna, in fantasy mine,
Is majesty's mystery—borne to be thine!

'Glazen Ticker'

[sixteen]

When ashen aspirations, *Lord of Hope*,
Me left a little lost, the worse for wear,
Thou wast a jolly good companion—nope,
A golden oldie—gleam that glinting stare!—
Who, antioxidant t' unruly heart,
Must glowing Grace beneficent impart,
Whene'er dat dratted Death, to think in throes,
Co-tenancy inviteth, I suppose!
Thou, *Architect of Love*, must spirit burn,
Igniting it abundantly, *en masse*—
So, I'll be at the pump, should'st thou return,
My glazen ticker up to top with gas!

Division throughout hist'ry hath its prints—
Some making apostolic ... others wince!

'The Proof'

seventeen

"Believest thou?" she's coy to quiz of him—
Whose int'rest, rather, focus on a limb
That peeketh, porcelain, beneath some wood:
She'd profit from an answer, if he could
Philosophy distil from reign of lust—
Th' arousal of his rasping resin's crust,
Which he, we know not wherefore, must construe
More credible than *kudos*, cogs in lieu!
"Believe I do!" he answers, tame and true
To sentiments he never thought he knew—
As eyes, ignoring hers, revert below
The wood his will is nail'd, to forgo...

"Thy God is good—enough to be aloof
To me, mere man for burning up, in proof!"

'Euphony's Encounter'

[eighteen]

There must, in Hope that grows, be dew—in rows
And rows of Love, for paucity of prose...
Thee, sweet artiste, I'm seeing fit to choose,
This Knight's to be companionship and muse—
Albeit hopes convening inner cells
Are neither what invincible compels,
Nor, swain salacious sucking in for Belle's
Unparallel'd persuasion, frankly tells...
Yet resurrection euphony will see
(Mature as *Kahlúa*'s Heavenly
Collusion with her mocktail I applaud)
In levity of loveliness, *Good Gourd*...

But he at issue—will he ever come,
To pat a mat, or slap a stolen drum?

'Falling Spirit, Tenderly'

How ought I, Amarita, just extol
The virtue of thy young, majestic soul?
Thou, Princess Sweet, art blushing when I look,
Misapprehending how a gentle brook
Of blue eyes, welling crystals never seen,
Should me reprove ... for ever having been!
Next day, I iterate thee walking by,
As, thee beholding, transigence I try
In thee, upon my sorrows to attract—
Thou, my remorse rewarding, smilest back!
Thus, Hope will make an offer, as I act,
Through this, my violation to retract:

One spirit, falling tenderly, a dove
Hath nectar now I needn't lose, to love!

'Super Woman'

[twenty]

A statue, temple, edifice of love—
I pray to her erection's wanton glove—
Whose subjugated student, sore enough
In nature's knot, hot bod to witness near,
'Neath husks of honey, happy would appear!
From lurking eyes, she's seeking to decline
Her tenderness, away from arching spine,
To bury breasts' inclusion in a top—
Lest hips, in panoplies of what she wear,
Tight clinging to her moist and fecund lair,
Succumb to sanction, willing spiel drop
Resistance—his to vanquish, hers to stop...

My *Super Woman*, eyes of stainless steel
Are witness to the weak ... who cling to zeal!

'Pearl'

[twenty-one]

Of skin so white, of flowing russet locks,
Of fingernails pink, to match her bra—
O'er which, in vain, the prettiest of frocks
May try to hide beneath what treasures are:
So do I on thee ponder, ne'er again
T' expend creation—Christen me a churl!—
When for another I would hold my pen,
Her thinking of how greater price the pearl...
But gone forever, never to return
Is she, who loved me back, of cheeky grin—
So, who am I, another's bridge to burn,
With whom to coalesce ought art begin?

How often caught betwixt I am, between
What love has brought to light ... and life has seen!

'Hungarian Queen'

[twenty-two]

Of Magyars marauding is monarchy mine
To perish for—paean for peahen a cock's
Enlightenment, sought in abundance divine ...
Mistaking her moonscape for love—on the rocks!
She wily, I willingly, once on a glance,
Must fall for that infamous face in a room—
When, through her, soliloquies learning to dance,
Became my cool *kismet*'s career, in bloom...
'Tis said that, in her tortured tongue, must a man
Burn up like an *ember* indwelling a grate;
Ye learn of me, cursing the fact that her fan
Must, spying her evidence, punish his pate!

In poignancy, skits such as this, though amazed,
A man best in bud nip ... before pen is raised!

'Down, Lucifer, Down!'

[twenty-three]

The Lord is my shepherd, in contrast with thee—
A wicked rapscallion, blackguard, and rake,
Whose dastardly plotting quite cleverly we
Got wise to, preferring that brimstony lake
To give but a miss—to partake with the Lord
Of diets diurnal (albeit one wag
Said after the first thousand years we'd get bored!)
Conjecture aside—for delusion to brag
Of fellowship 'twixt His Good Lordship and I,
Is futile—this brute I'll be muting art *thou*:
To witness, 'tis written where truth and way lie—
Best fall on ya fours, better start begging now!

For, ambulating Death's dark dell, I shall
Continue feeding Lucy ... Chum and Pal!

'Love Cat'

[twenty-four]

Benighted Earth, drab, desolate, and dark,
Is home to seeds my solitude hath sown;
Requiting Love is hard when Hope is stark—
And so, I task a weary barque, alone...
Then, momentary spectre, small and slick,
Ascending into space, to grace my scene,
Is keen, and quick, and quiveringly chic—
Proclivity's epitome, my Queen!
Purrfection paw'd and whisker'd, I can sense
My feline soul enamour'd of surprise,
In ecstasy of agony immense—
To see thee, gone, on phantom's inner eyes!

Love cat—a tonic!—maketh man of wuss,
His furry fortune finding ... in a puss!

'Narcissus, Pauper, Prince'

[twenty-five]

Am I, whom sifting Fortune will ignore,
Perforce to feel sorry, sad, or sore,
When, all about me, others, by the score,
Know better reason, more to coo or caw,
Than I? Quick covert errors, in the Law,
I query—what's this life I'm living for?
Regretting broken noses, broken jaw
Not—God is ever willing, I am sure,
And wouldn't want me knocking on a door
In Heaven, mirror seeking, lest *rapport*
In apparitions, echoing a flaw
I'm giving up, should see the wild boar

Inside my soul—His Poor, on whom, in store,
Doth wait a Princess ... feminal and raw!

'Desire's Dear Dream'

[twenty-six]

Prosaic doth a moment seem to deem
Desire stirring in a womb, whose groom
Frivolities of eloquence would scheme
Within a status quo, within a room—
Lest thou, now spinning verily a dream,
On Love's probation, will a creaming loom
To settle stream of consciousness, her team
Then steaming in, to beam it up—on Zoom!
God, I do not imbibe, nor do I smoke—
No smoking, 'tis the sermon of the day—
Sometimes I try to push and prod and poke
Machines into a prophet: Safe to say,

Desire's dream was dear, until she came
T' entrench "*a lousy lay*"—too blest to blame!

'The End of the Affair'

[twenty—seven]

Thou show'rest, waxing, waning, in the dark,
Till, left to grace the Hill of Love, an heir
Hath not a hope in Hades—to be stark,
Once more do I call loving thee despair...
For there doth beat, beneath a heathen heart,
A snapshot of our state of play, in loans
And mortgages—must Hope be torn apart,
Refuting sweet devotion, via bones?
Now tinnitus is ringing through these ears,
A legacy of contumacious tones—
This sentimental lover's in arrears,
For severing endeavour ... all he owns!

From ev'ry new beginning, love is penn'd—
Until what once was winning's on the mend!

'If that Tyrant thou Prefer'

[twenty-eight]

What art, what intrigue, is my Dove above?
Upon my heart doth wrench her laughter gone;
A splint'ring, splicing dart hath cleft, in love,
Impressionism's mart her smile's on...
Take Satan, if that tyrant thou prefer—
Yea, wrench the wrench primeval from its socket!—
And if thou lean towards his face of fur,
Then put it in its place, inside my locket—
Oh, wherefore not? E'en that old rabid cur
Needs beareth burnish'd brass within his pocket!
Still, know thou this, attend me clearly, rightly:
Wert thou but mine, a diamond polish'd nightly,

I'd whet mine appetite upon thy stone—
In light left to beglisten ... like a bone!

'Holy Mackerel!'

[twenty-nine]

Love covereth a multitude of sins:
'Tis written in the pamphlet I peruse—
Reversals in pecuniary wins
There making up, for modern man, Good News!
I like them pretty pictures—I must think
The one that's counting fishies, loaves, and droves
A fave: Hey, don't those basket cases stink?
And tell, where are your godforsaken stoves?
Oh, woe betide you, small fry, if ye fail
To double-cross that fisherman, to net
Days left to praise as *sushi*, Holy Grail
A misappropriation of regret...

Go live it up in Heaven, piscine teams:
      Good luck! Sleep tight!
            Sweet dreams, my love, sweet dreams!

'Acme of Creation'

[thirty]

What cause have I, O fickle, faithless lover,
Thy sex to venerate above the other?
True, thou hast neither need for sword, nor mace,
To stick it up thy satin, silk, or lace,
Nor doth behind that pretty, precious face
Reside a mind whose guile, preconceived,
Be thought belittled, just to be believed...
Cool, calculating, showing scant remorse,
Thou art a cat—cruel, merciless thy claws
Thou must retract, before, beneath thy paws,
Th' ingenuous mouse, a seeker after cheese,
Is left to masticate thy perfidies!

Thou, Woman, art the acme of creation—
Or should I spell one letter better, hey Hon?

'Fantasy's Possession'

[thirty-one]

Romance, to bakers on a beach, may be
Imagination's dance, in potency...
Thy body lissome, succulent, is spann'd
In glory, tann'd, demanding, on the sand—
Each peek or plaudit plann'd to countermand
A loitering exposure to a doubt,
Lest pleasure be requited, in a drought...
Thee lying there do I, in stealth, survey,
To contemplate, in senses' disarray,
The scantiness of hope to harbour what
My fantasy, rebuttal knowing not,
Would extricate, in loveliness, from cloth!

If some would say, thou much not leave unshown,
Yet something doth imagination own!

'Jealous Coup de Grâce'

[thirty-two]

Thou dost, on whitest squares of black, attack
In games from which may be no coming back:
If unto thee He be, in kind, disposed—
Thy God, who thee doth nurture, in demence—
Who on thee Earthly sentence hath imposed,
By dint of quite divine benevolence:
Then do I hope, His wrath, in roots of ire,
T' inherit be not thine, nor to inspire—
He pity take, before He seek to sell
Thee, to disgrace those pretty pits of Hell...
For here, on Earth, thou must politely tread,
Or suffer slightly more, when thou art dead:

Yea, on thee doth inexorably wait
His gentle, jealous *coup de grâce* ... Checkmate!

'Flaw's Perfection'

[thirty-three]

The face, in one swell thinker's judgment lent,
Is surely a reflection of the soul:
Yet now, methinks, brute arrows Cupid sent,
Embracing thee, forsake the Golden Bowl...
Still, verily be admiration due
To thee, to see a gap, in dental debt,
Whose evidence, in *mores* hugging two,
May Hope embrace, delicious in regret...
Yea, I must recognize thee in a crowd,
Which, ever since adjourning, hath a way
To glimpse, betwixt thy teeth, my love allow'd—
Beyond thy dental cortex, safe to say...

In beauty everlasting, on my brain,
Is flaw's perfection ... transcendental lane!

'Recollection Haunting'

[thirty-four]

Thou art, for whom my heart doth beat, unsure
That somehow loving, from a fickle fan,
Did whisk thee up to Paradise, before
He up and went, to God knows where, to pan
Thy golden soul—forever his for grieving,
One he never felt again, to lose
A love, in her, not half as bad as leaving—
Songs she couldn't sing, in sunny hues...
Though me not once deceiving, disappointing,
Haughty heights must cast asunder thee:
Which recollection hateful, heinous, haunting,
Dumb accomplice mine shall ever be—

When, if to enter Heaven He allow,
Shall this fiend one sweet angel welcome: thou.

'Art on a Horse'

[thirty-five]

Equestrienne so proud, art on a horse,
That, cantering its bold and bonny course,
Is crewing Love's blue battlefield—truer
Knight she waits on ... for King Pin, to skewer!
Of many victims seen, are victors fewer,
In panoply's calamity, perverse,
T' entrust her minion's *manna* to manure—
For thou, in Dragon's Blood though His t' immerse,
Shalt meet an even stronger potion's brewer,
Whose name, betimes, came pithy to rehearse,
By scholar, poet, visionary, wooer—
Committing now to palace, now to sewer!

In *armour* haughty is thy Fate obscure—
Forgetting who is best to mate: *"Amour"*.

'Angel of Desire'

[thirty-six]

Doth Love accompany the word *desire*?
Methought thee priceless, pristine, perfect, pure—
But now, *O Meretrix*, doth thee attire
A putrid, poxy mantle of manure!
Did Goodness thee conceive, to undergo
Transition to creation of effects
Degenerate—which must on video
Excite mass perturbation, via sex?
What devil, what pariah made thee fall,
That thou should'st quit thy snug supernal perch?
That thou should'st expectation so appal—
And Heaven's proud construction so besmirch?

'Tis metamorphosis both sad and strange,
When butterflies to caterpillars change!

'Beauty's Curse'

[thirty-seven]

How long must tarry here her vapid stain?

I linger long enough, in beauty's curse,

To wax, in hope, that she might rapid wane—

To put to bed this piquancy I nurse!

Good Lord! I would not darkness know, nor death,

And, like poor Jonah, trapp'd in fish's core,

Seek rescue from thy bright and breezy breath—

To be again spat out upon a shore

Where lust's imperative shall not bestir,

Nor importunity of senses shake,

And each and ev'ry hapless hope of her

Shall, bleeding, billow its macabre wake!

For love, unfounded, vain and noxious proved,

Is best, post-haste, uprooted—and removed.

'From Time's Beginning'

[thirty-eight]

From Time's beginning thee I have adored,
And from thy soul's inception I thee knew;
In love for thee shall be my soul's reward,
And radiant e'er shall be my being's hue:
Thou shalt me comfort in life's cold duress,
And be for life's disease sufficient balm;
And thou—in turn—shalt care for my caress,
Each interloper shall I swift disarm:
That thou should'st know: thou art my love supreme,
The One I ne'er shall squander, nor regret;
The One in whom I trust, of whom I dream—
The One, in hope, I, countenancing, met:

Yea, thou shalt ever in a heart reside,
True, truant Lover, loving cannot hide.

'Real Meal Deal'

[thirty-nine]

O hero hung high—naughty, haughty tricks
Thee putting up for shutting up ... a fix!
That sober, sweet coagulation, blood
Superior—lest madding, milling chicks,
So probing, chew on cheap Jehovah's cud:
Be cheerier, they say, try riffs or licks,
To minimize what's molten, in the mud!
Yet, were it mine, that Sickly Sea of Swill
T' admonish, but a second on my hand,
I should indict a peach, for having nil—
To spill such slaughter, sinking in the sand...

Thy sap, 'tis dripping, soft enough to steal,
For common wealth, me ready to reveal
The gist of Jove ... that real meal deal!

'Thy Better Judgment'

[forty]

O Lord of host and ghost, this toast I do
Link up with Retribution's Buccaneer,
T' invoke the Love of God, that sad *adieu*
Beginning with each retrospective tear...
The Wicked One's a worry—sure he is!
Look out, lest, on the loose, he lure lambs,
Thy fellow doting parents, kids in prams,
With all the broken hearted, making His...
Lest butter be my date, unwittingly,
On cells of grey to swim St Joseph's Lake,
So let due Hope consent, befitting me,
T' accept thy better judgment ... like a snake!

No condemnation in our God, they say,
Though souls will burn forever ... and a day.

'Jupiter'

[forty-one]

'Tis well now spoken, Jupiter, of thee,
Though storms conform unholy chemistry
To rise above that sacred weaponry
Of mettle's inner worth: Thy virgin birth
Doth prey on sunken salt, resurgent death
Might quite belie that outer shell, whose stealth
Preserveth thee—as frozen, fractious fruit
Now fallen, free'd from bondage, reaping youth...
In Paradise alive, *O Prince of Earth*,
To reign as David, bearing sling and stone,
And living, wholly stripp'd of flesh and bone—
Thy love doth hope, in vain, to stain my own...

For where I lay my Heart and Soul, *forsooth*,
Is where I lay my Light, my Love, my Truth!

'Queen Kunti'

[forty-two]

May stars incline to shine, now thou be near
To him—a heart by chemistry made quick:
A cup of *lassi*, transcendental tear
From Heaven, conjured milky white and thick,
He's willing to endear—for thou his spear
Fell makest swell, by strange, erotic trick...
Thou, *Apple of his Eye*, juice, pulp, and core,
Art *raison* for his *être*, *idée fixe*,
Replenishment of boxes, all the more
Exquisite, for replenishment of ticks—
When, taking naked cake, six thousand licks
Insinuate Queen Kunti's bushy mix

To snatch relief in relish-sodden dew ...
Adorning lush the lash of lavish shrew!

'Sugar Hill'

[forty-three]

Somewhere there be a place called 'Sugar Hill'—
'Twixt mustard bread and wine, I heard it said—
If thou should'st be my pane, I'd be thy sill,
And bleed for thee as seldom liking bled...
Whose potion hath a notion to improve
Love's hardship, full of beans, disdaining hose?
To entertain thee, I'd yet enter groove,
And readily accommodate my rose;
Or else: accommodated be, remove
Linguistic cunning, candidly propose
On Sugar Hill a meeting made in love—
'Twixt errant eagle, and his saving dove...

Where Man his marrow's issue doth belie—
In ecstasy to live, in love to die!

'Lovers & Poets'

[forty-four]

In Love, thinking on thee, my soul is at Peace;
In Grace—how amazing—my being is whole:
Vexation of spirit will yield, then cease—
As Hope's gravid mare, contemplating her foal...
Eternity, spark of thy flickering flame,
Is dwelling on thee when its paeans rehearse
Vitality's wellspring—such as it became
To quench and to satiate; musing, I nurse
Thy gentle propensities, beauteous form,
Committing to follow but whither thou go:
To dance in a fire, to sleep in a storm—
To bridge living waters upwelling below!

May Lovers and Poets now contemplate thee,
For whom breath is drawn, till they fail to be.

'Spotless Lap'

[forty-five]

I cede to recitation of my years
In vagabondage unto gravity—
And hear no loud applause, resounding cheers,
To deafen middle-aged depravity...
Appear do things to me, six decades grown—
A twisted, mangled wreck on pity's shores—
As if I, scarce one moment having known,
Should like, in sempiternity, its pause:
To breathe in air, both oxygen unslurr'd,
And nitrogen, to blanket me in gas
Less toxic than a choice, chew'd, chaliced Word—
Oblivious of need to stomach Mass...

And yet I dare to hope, to flee this trap—
Undress'd, in pieces, on His spotless lap!

'A Pot of Little Songs'

[forty-six]

Is Love enough? I'm sinking! To be sold
Submission fogging up the ghost of eyes,
This Knight, as once for thee one truly bold,
Would bow t' amend the truth—with all its lies!
And yet, unto thy glory, I should stir
A pot of little songs, leave love to lock
Elysium abuzz, if not apurr,
Ere one who isn't welcome, prone to mock,
Should sell the sea I sail on, afloat
With boats I bury deep in buxom waves—
Since thou, so nearly here, at mercy's throat,
Art symbiotic with hypnotic staves!

Howbeit, knowing thee, I shall not run
Too far, till hope is lost ... and loss hath won!

'From Russia with Lust'

[forty-seven]

O Lena, Lust Incorporated, thou
St Petersburg hast left discons'late now!
No cosmonaut is needed to declare
Allegiance of his gander to thy goose:
Adjust he must, in vain, his orbs, prepare
To case the place thou wast, now on the loose...
For thou didst leave to grieve a stratosphere
Of brethren angels, born to seek allure
Of molehill moist, men making mountain, mere
To spy, in *perestroika*, one mole fewer!
Yea, lost to *dasvidaniya*s, fare-thee-wells,
I, helpless, in a panegyric's spells,

Connect to lines on pages, mine t' invent
Thy nectar's plea contagious—innocent!

'At Reign's End'

[forty-eight]

If words were spoken, reawoken I
Must acquiesce to silence, at reign's end,
Protruding brooding fingers to the sky—
In homage to that fairly faultless friend
Indwelling loft on high ye can but shy,
Defiance buying, hope to pawn, or lend…
If I became, still am, and live to tell
Quick anecdotes, till ghost be given up,
'Twere best to grin and bear despair in Hell—
For, ever one for savouring, I sup
On Love of Light, returning to the well
To cradle wafers, lest contrition's cup

Count Dracula, swig bloody, bleating dew—
So lost on one who never knew he knew!

'Grand Illusions'

[forty-nine]

A mouse am I, my prison's port in sloth:
So trapp'd by knots thought Gordian, I do
Salvation's leave select from grapes of wrath—
And grand delinquencies, now tried and true!
How is this God so galling, to require
Deception grand, for making grand deceit,
A mouse's life worth having lived, inspire
A mouse to take steps, with poetic feet?
As Fate would frame, on cheese I must be fed—
As pate proclaim: a foodstuff I should choose
Reluctantly, for, taken from its bed
Of wormwood, sweating tears of morning dews,

I, rodent ruing, rude release request
From grand illusions ... messy, ah, and blest!

'Josie'

[fifty]

Vehicular we sat, thy temple close
To mine, mere to be near thee hard to take;
As, equally, emotion for thee, Jose,
In fingers moving moist, arose to ache!
My Dream thou art, my Queen, my Goddess chaste,
Whom mortal man may covet, if repelt;
Yet I, one perfect fit to find, am placed
Before thee, my Cathartic Angel, felt...
True, I must keep mine eyes upon the prize,
Albeit one not easy to requite—
For retinae and irises are lies,
If, out of mind, two hearts be out of sight...

This man thought Love too far from him, to heed—
Whom, on her waiting, finding him, she free'd.

'She'

[fifty—one]

She is my Light, my Love, my Truth—my spoor
Shall follow whither she doth make her path,
Upon no other gazing—*strewth!*—before
She hath her love extinguish'd, from my heart...
In darkest moments I have ask'd my God
If He doth me yet fondly countenance;
If comfort I shall find in staff and rod,
Or banish'd be from Love's aloof expanse:
But eyes do sparkle, freckles smile, too,
Her soul aglow, to balance mine on heat—
Permitting Hope to kindle there anew,
Her patch to snatch in vict'ry, from defeat!

Yet, if *her* love be *His* to rude deny,
Then *He* be ignominious—not I!

'Love's Patient'

[fifty-two]

How long I lie awake! A pretty face
Hath made its pledge to, *Fleur de Lys*, return;
How singular she is! Dismay I chase—
To gild her lily, till a silver fern
Intoxicate infatuation, brace
For days of living lovingly I earn...
If hope, however happily we meet,
Succumb to her delusion, like the wind
Invisibly deflating, born to cheat
Division, in the sinner, or the sinn'd
Against—so let paralysis unseat
Love's Patient, broken, baffled, bent, and binn'd...

Who hath the final Word is ever He—
No patient claiming bragging rights, like me!

'Going Out with Jesus'

[fifty-three]

Consider, Heaven's Maiden, my request:
Consider me escorting, on a date;
Consider how I thee polite address'd ...
In venting my nativity, to mate!
True, thou didst acquiesce, to offer brash
Thy condescension, for me to allow
Love to exhaust, on thy behalf, my cash,
To venerate instead a human cow—
Thee taking to a show, wherein, *entr'acte*,
I went out on a limb, and held thy hoof—
Which member thou didst, withering, retract,
And move to pastures meaner, more aloof!

Thou, Bovine Belle, wast, like charisma cross'd,
Then "going out with Jesus"—to my cost!

'Four Wills and a Way'

[fifty-four]

O Heav'nly Father, not my will, but thine
Be done, for of the two mine's wilting more;
Thou knowest best, good Dr Frankenstein,
With whom I do enjoy such close *rapport*...
The Evil, Adamantine, I have tried
To show the Way to Heaven, by my Truth—
Though I, in whom redemption doth reside,
Am somewhat loath to go there, in my youth...
'Tis strange, howbeit, dost not think, that they
Thy monster mild and meek must mix with thee?
Such ignorance, methinketh, doth betray
Appreciation minimal—for me!

Still, Popsy, not thy will, but mine be done ...
Oops, did that line again—forgive thy Son!

'Heart Song'

[fifty-five]

So many's the Woman of *wannabe* worth,
But thou, as no other, excellest them all:
Hey, custom a cord for my trachea's girth,
And gladsome, in throes, at thy feet I shall fall!
A song in the heart of Divinity's Child;
An aria on the soft breezes of dusk;
A melody happen'd on, gentle and mild;
A kernel of loveliness, shedding her husk—
In *chiaroscuro* 'tis clothing the ground,
T' unveil a form silhouetted in love,
Which I, devotee of felicity's mound,
Incline deep to worship … wet feminal glove!

Th' impossible dream hath one name—it is thine—
And dreaming it dreamt in communion with mine!

'Evolution Gemma'

[fifty–six]

So Gemma hath her daddy, he his spouse—
Just possibly they too may speak of stock—
But, if thou would'st go back in time, thy nous
Must needs conclude thy rellie was a rock!
Exceeding sore, relieved of locks of love
I am, engaging birdlife in a tweet—
Of wren, owl, eagle, raven, turtle dove …
From art in fancy flight, one man's conceit!
Is Man to Bird superior? On wing
Our feather'd friends hegemonize the sky—
Whence avian propensities will sing:
"We'll infiltrate as *seraphim*, to ply

Your Earth evolving…" God made Woman to
Be Man's best Bird … if only Gemma knew!

'Lioness of Snow'

[fifty—seven]

My Little Friend, am I to joyous end
My days on Earth, companion unto thee?
So feminine a feline, I contend,
Hath never graced its surface—purringly!
Now reach I forth to stroke her, 'twixt my thighs
A lovely, luscious, breathing ball of fur,
And realize much greater is my prize
Than what is wise—gold, frankincense, or myrrh...
She, Lioness of Snow, their wild Queen,
Upon whom I could rest my gaze, in love,
Eternally—as though a child seen
By her own Papa, watching from above—

Doth light up creation, illumine my quilt,
Her ginger eyes gleaming ... with innocent guilt!

'Sixth Commandment'

[fifty—eight]

Man saith that *nice* yet three-and-twenty times
Its meaning have, at least in Saxon tongue;
But many are those slips, betwixt them crimes,
On which are dopish, dumb descriptors hung:
Still thou—thee I do not for so inept,
Nay: keen, cold, cruel, yea: vain, vexatious view,
That I should thee give soporific cause
To make but do with solipsistic flaws,
O'er which oft-times must hard have moping wept
Surveyors seeking *thee*, he planting *you*...
Mmm, I have in mine heart an hoping kept,
That, thou and I, together twenty-two

Nice milky white and wicked ways were giv'n—
To be thy friend, six making out of sev'n.

'Soaring Eagle, Noble Wolf'

[fifty-nine]

Creation, howsoever it became,
Doth boast of beast both beautiful and bright,
Amongst which latter hot debate doth flame—
Germane to who is wrong ... and who is right!
'Tis secret not that noble wolf of yore
Hath given rise, through agency of Man,
To each and ev'ry genome-bearing paw
Of puppy, doting dog and bitch began...
But lo, look up! Perhaps ye wonder why
Fab eagles soar, superior, above—
I put it down to God, that clever guy,
Who's weighing truth, for giving life to love!

A lighthouse shineth, noble, through the fog—
Though void to wolf evolve ... then back to dog!

'Sun Goddess'

[sixty]

Fantabulous thy breasts, whose heathen hips
Do rob of breath, in seismic, cosmic class—
This man would live his life to love thy lips,
To pen an ode, in candour, on thine arse!
Thy buttonhole permitteth not a ring
To compromise God's chemistry conceived—
Which luminary's Truth I thought a thing
In doubt, till I saw thee ... and I believed!
How might a man requite that vital Love,
About which thine whole being doth rotate?
How might he Lust's high, holy pow'r improve—
To see thee close, in proud, primeval state?

Thou art, indeed, creation never bested—
For after God created thee, He rested.

"It isn't the End of the World!"
I hear them, so sunnily, say:
"It isn't the Start of it, either!
Just let us grow honey—we pray..."

And so, I, vacating the stage,
Sing sonnets, inside, on a page!

The End

www.ingramcontent.com/pod-product-compliance
Lightning Source LLC
Chambersburg PA
CBHW031235120626
46545CB00003B/1134